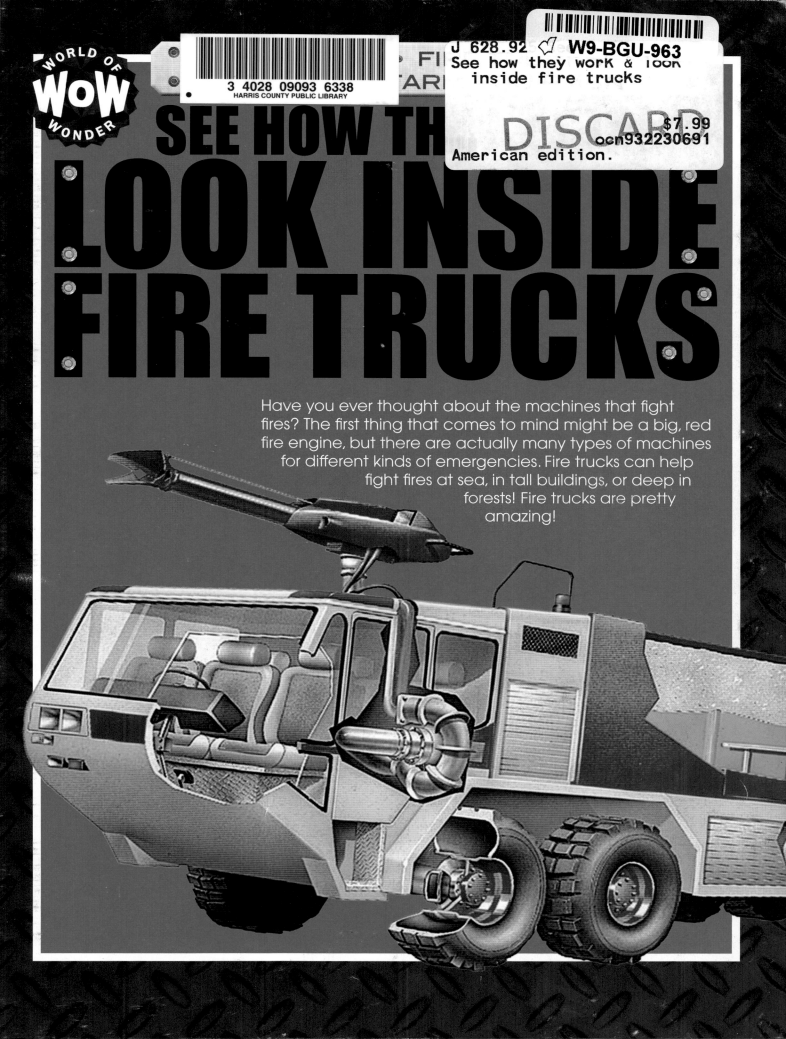

SEE HOW THEY LOOK INSIDE FIRE TRUCKS

Have you ever thought about the machines that fight fires? The first thing that comes to mind might be a big, red fire engine, but there are actually many types of machines for different kinds of emergencies. Fire trucks can help fight fires at sea, in tall buildings, or deep in forests! Fire trucks are pretty amazing!

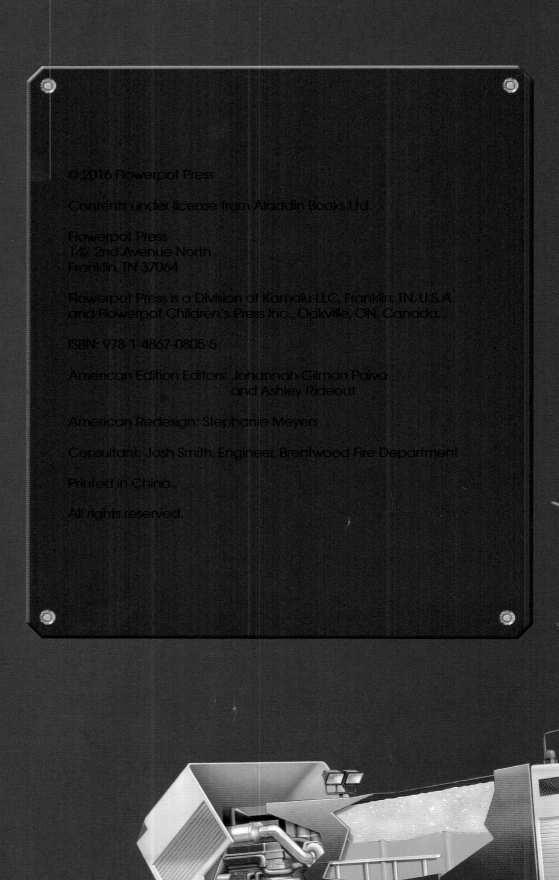

© 2016 Flowerpot Press

Contents under license from Aladdin Books Ltd.

Flowerpot Press
142 2nd Avenue North
Franklin, TN 37064

Flowerpot Press is a Division of Kamalu LLC, Franklin, TN, U.S.A.
and Flowerpot Children's Press Inc., Oakville, ON, Canada.

ISBN: 978-1-4867-0805-5

American Edition Editors: Johannah Gilman Paiva
                                and Ashley Rideout

American Redesign: Stephanie Meyers

Consultant: Josh Smith, Engineer, Brentwood Fire Department

Printed in China.

TABLE OF CONTENTS

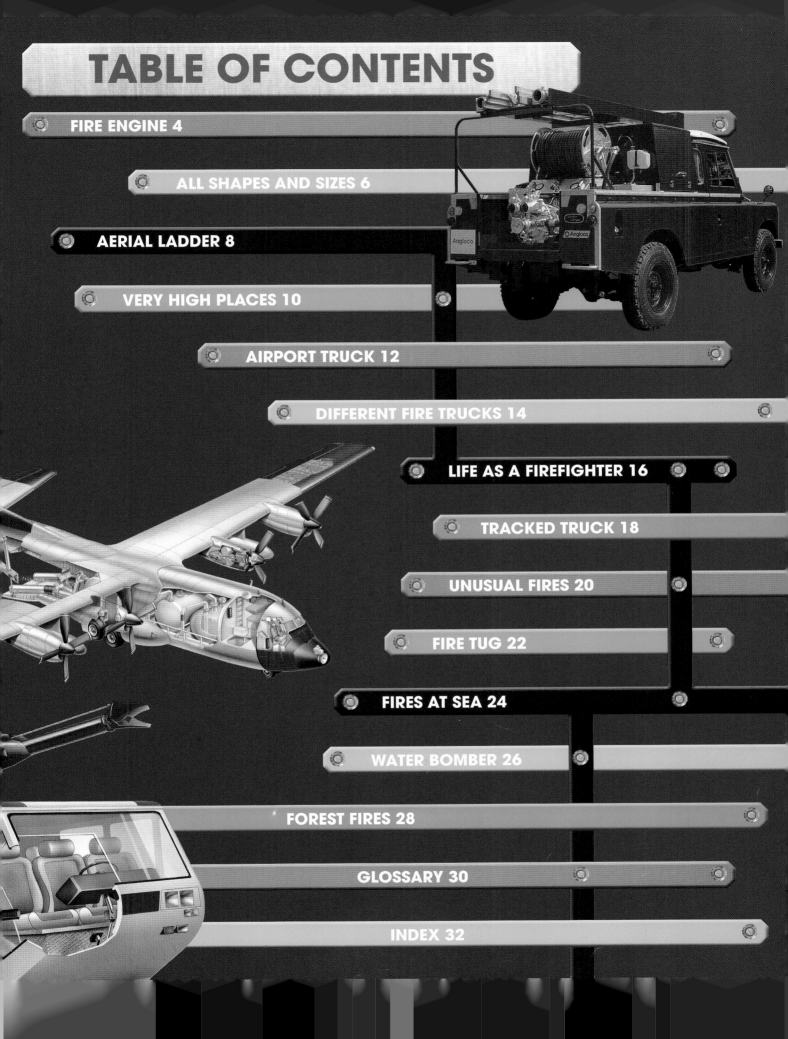

FIRE ENGINE

Fire engines race down streets to get to a blaze quickly. Their lights flash and sirens blare to clear a path through traffic. The truck carries a team of firefighters, and it also holds all the equipment they need to help in many situations. This includes a big tank full of water—it holds enough water to fill over 40 bathtubs! The water is pumped out through the large hoses attached to the truck.

Deck gun
This special water outlet is a high-capacity water jet. It shoots water out the top of the engine and can spray a stream a long distance to the top of a building.

Ladder
Ladders are used to rescue people from high buildings—or to get a cat out of a tree!

Equipment
Fire engines carry hoses, lights, medical equipment, breathing equipment (see page 16), and

Control panel
The control panel has many buttons and levers that are used to operate the pump that pushes water through

Wheel
The wheels on the engine have to be thick and strong to support the weight of all the water and equipment in

This fire engine (right) has many outlets for hoses to attach in order to tap into the water supply in the engine.

Jumpseat

Four to six firefighters ride in this compartment, ready to jump out when they reach the fire.

Cab

The driver sits in the front to steer the truck. The rest of the firefighters sit behind him or her in the cab.

Siren and lights

The flashing lights and noisy siren warn people that the fire engine is coming.

Engine

The engine provides the power to drive the fire truck. Fire truck engines can have up to 600 horsepower—that is three times as powerful as a car engine!

ALL SHAPES AND SIZES

Fire trucks haven't always been big and red like those you might see on the street today. The first fire trucks had to be small enough to be pulled by horses. Some trucks today may be smaller with just a water tank and ladder, while others might be green or yellow with lots of equipment.

STEAM ENGINE

Early fire trucks were powered by steam (left and below). Water was heated in a boiler to produce steam. This gave the truck's pump the power to push water through the hoses. At the time these were in use, vehicle motors did not exist. These early steam engines had to be drawn to the fire by a team of horses!

Seat
Firefighters would sit here to direct the horses to the fire.

Boiler
The metal boiler got very hot when working to make enough steam to power the hoses.

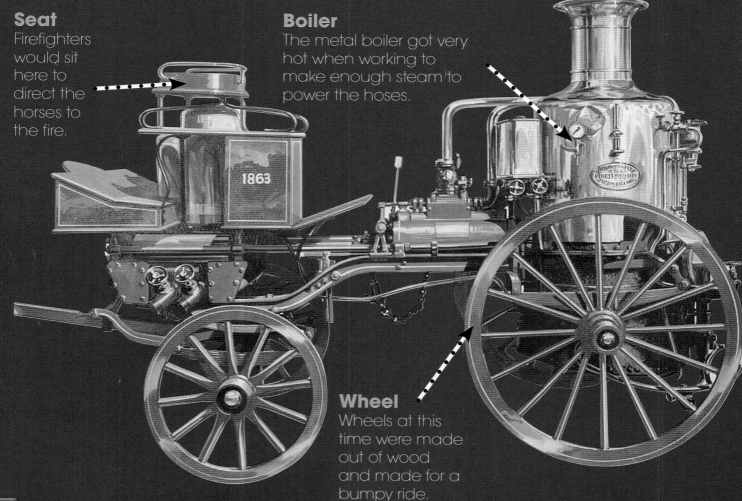

Wheel
Wheels at this time were made out of wood and made for a bumpy ride.

FIREFIGHTING HISTORY

The first organized fire brigade was in ancient Rome. The firefighters were equipped with hand pumps, ladders, buckets, and pickaxes. They also had blankets to protect themselves from heat. In 1982, a fire in Borneo lasted for 10 months. It was only put out when heavy rain started to fall.

TODAY'S TRUCKS

This tiny British fire engine (left) carries ladders, hoses, and two firefighters. It can get to fires down very narrow streets or can be used for off-road search and rescue missions.

OIL REFINERY FIRE TRUCK

This small fire engine (right) works at an oil refinery. Because oil burns quickly, this truck needs to be able to get to a fire with extra speed.

STANDARD FIRE TRUCK

Standard fire trucks (right) are big because they have to carry lots of equipment. Don't be fooled by its yellow color! Some fire engines are yellow so that they are more easily spotted at night.

AERIAL LADDER

Sometimes firefighters need to reach fires in high places. To do this, they use a long ladder. This fire truck is as tall as 20 people standing on top of each other! It is hinged in the middle so that it can turn tight corners. Even though it is very long, this fire truck can drive down winding streets because its back can swing around.

Ladder
When the truck gets to the fire, the ladder extends to reach the flames. The ladder can also help firefighters reach people stuck on high floors in a building.

Turntable
This huge ladder is attached to a turntable. The turntable can spin the ladder in a complete circle. The end of the ladder can also be moved up and down by a control lever!

Stabilizer
These special legs prevent the fire truck from falling over when the heavy ladder is used.

Cab

Hose

The ladder has a hose at the end of it. Water runs up the ladder, and a firefighter can use this hose to put out fires in high places.

Rear cab

Trucks that can bend in the middle are called "tiller trucks." From here, a firefighter can steer the fire truck wheels at the back. This helps the fire truck to turn very tight corners.

Equipment stores

Firefighters need a lot of equipment to put out a fire. This fire truck has enough space under the ladder to store all the gear they need, like oxygen tanks, extra hoses, saws, goggles, and airbags.

SNOWY CONDITIONS

Sometimes things like snow make it hard to get the engine close to a building. When this happens, a long ladder can help firefighters reach an emergency.

VERY HIGH PLACES

It is important for fire engines to be equipped with tall ladders because sometimes fires happen in tall buildings. The water jets also have to be strong enough to shoot far into the air to reach the far away blaze.

LADDER RESCUE

When there is a fire in a very tall building, firefighters climb up a long ladder to help the people at the top of the building back down to safety (left).

DROPPING IN

Sometimes, even the longest ladder is not long enough. If this happens, firefighters may have to climb up the side of a building to reach a blaze (right).

HIGH HOSES

The hose on the end of a ladder lets firefighters spray water at flames that are far beyond the range of hoses on the ground (left).

Platform
The platform is wide enough for four people to stand on.

OUT THE WINDOW

This firefighter (above) will use the control panel in front of him to raise the platform high into the air to reach people at a window or roof of a building.

GOING UP...

This fire truck (below) does not have a standard ladder. Instead, it has a platform on the end of a long arm where a firefighter can ride. This platform can reach as high as an aerial ladder (see page 9). This platform gives a solid space for people to step onto when climbing out the window of a burning building.

Cab

Stabilizer

AIRPORT TRUCK

Fires at airports can be very dangerous. Disasters could happen in just a few seconds, because aircraft fuel burns very easily. When an airport fire truck arrives at a fire, it covers the blaze with a thick blanket of foam. Fire-fighting foam is developed specifically to extinguish flammable liquids. Foam is used because water would not stop aircraft fuel from burning. The truck is always on alert, because planes are always landing at busy airports.

Pipes
These pipes carry the foam from the tank to the cannon.

Foam cannon
A firefighter aims this foam cannon at the fire. Using it, a plane can be completely covered with fire-fighting foam in just a few seconds!

Cab
The big windows give the firefighters a good view of the fire. The cab also has bright lights

Wheel
This truck needs to be able to go from zero to 50 miles per hour (80.5 kilometers) in less than 35 seconds, so its wheels have to be durable

AIMING ABOVE

Foam cannons (right) can move to aim at a plane high in the air or on the runway. Sometimes it can take more than one engine to put out a fire.

Foam tank
Foam is stored in a huge tank inside the airport truck. From here, a powerful pump forces foam out through the foam cannon.

Engine
Airport trucks need very powerful engines to drive the truck at high speeds and power the pump.

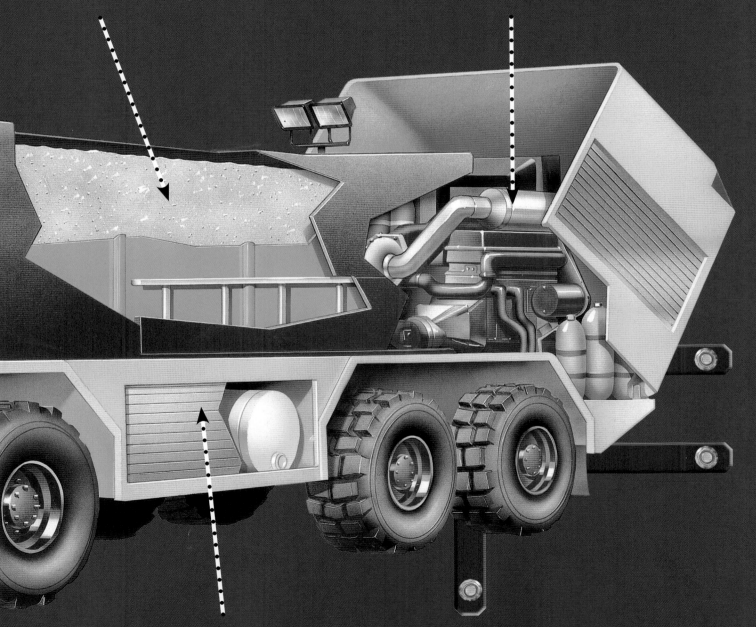

Equipment
The airport truck has equipment that the firefighters might need to rescue people from a plane. This includes ladders and breathing equipment.

DIFFERENT FIRE TRUCKS

Fire stations are prepared with many different kinds of equipment and trucks for the types of emergencies they might encounter. Towns with large forest areas need to have a truck able to travel on rough ground and between trees, while airport trucks need foam that can put out chemical fires.

RESCUE TRUCK

Not all emergencies are fires. This truck (right) has a crane to help lift heavy objects. It also carries equipment to rescue people trapped in cars, or even underground.

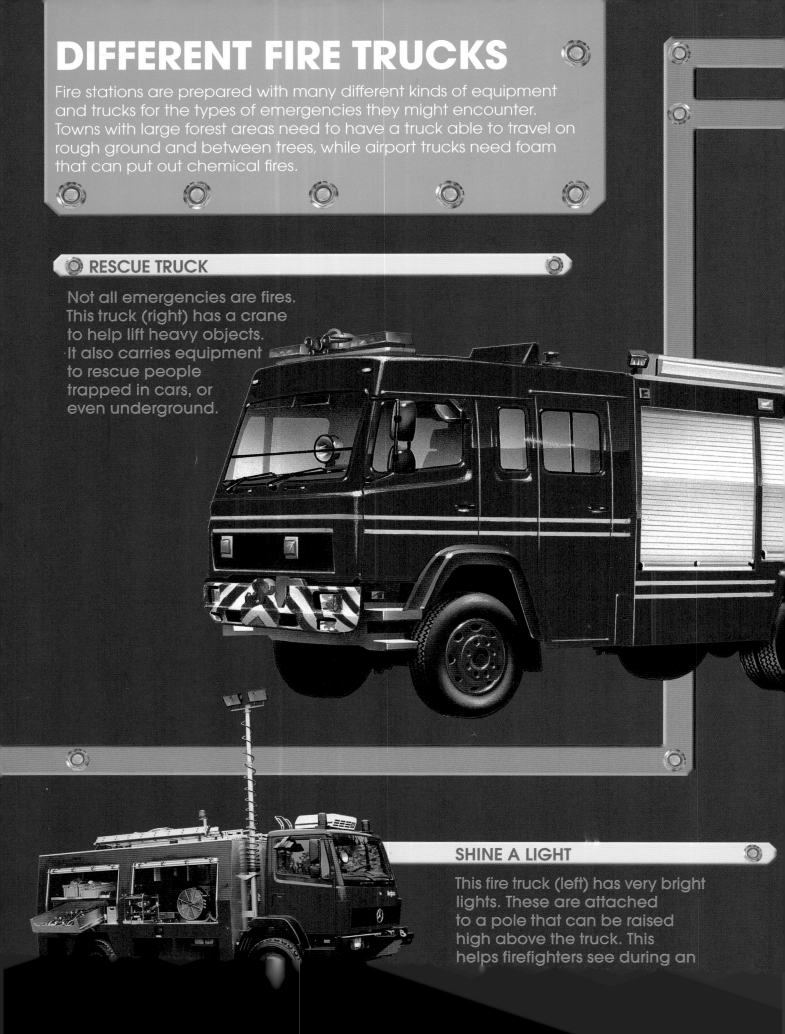

SHINE A LIGHT

This fire truck (left) has very bright lights. These are attached to a pole that can be raised high above the truck. This helps firefighters see during an

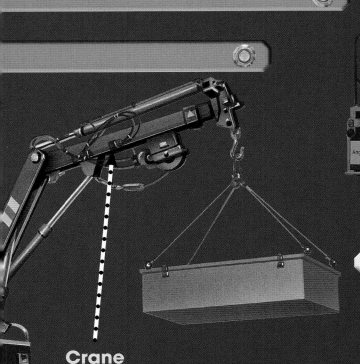

Crane

Stabilizer

OFF-ROAD TRUCKS

This fire truck (above) is specially made to drive over rough ground. It carries a small water tank and also has a pump that can take water from lakes or ponds.

COMMAND CAB

Some fires are very big and need many firefighters to put them out. To help direct such operations, a fire chief uses a special truck (below). This has a cab at the rear that acts as a command center.

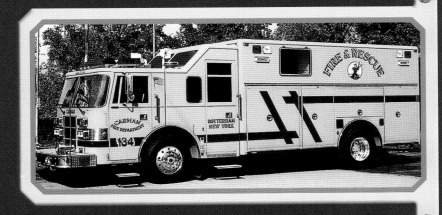

EXTRA FOAM

For very big fires, extra foam may be needed. The foam carrier (right) carries enough spare foam to help put out the largest fires.

LIFE AS A FIREFIGHTER

Firefighting is a job that takes specialized training. Not only do the firefighters need to be physically fit to handle the rough conditions they will encounter, but they also have to learn about fire chemistry and physics as well as firefighting techniques, investigation procedures, and emergency medical care. The firefighters live in the station during their duty shift, which usually lasts 24 hours. Once off duty, they are allowed to go home.

ON STANDBY

A lot of a firefighter's time is spent waiting for the next emergency. If the alarm sounds when they are eating (left), they have to leave their food.

INTO ACTION

Firefighters need to act quickly when the alarm sounds. Sometimes, they slide down a pole (right) to get to their fire trucks as quickly as possible. Sliding down the pole is a faster way to get down to the bottom floor than taking the stairs. Every second counts!

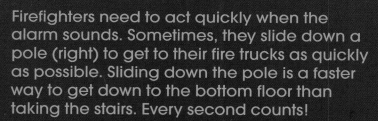

SAFE BREATHING

Smoke injures more people than fire itself. This is why breathing equipment is so important in helping to fight fires and rescuing people trapped in a blaze. Firefighters protect themselves from smoke and fumes by wearing equipment (left) that gives them air to breathe.

CLEANING UP

Sometimes, firefighters may have to clean up dangerous chemicals. To do this, they wear special suits (above) that are designed to keep out the dangerous chemicals. They also use oxygen tanks to prevent breathing in any harmful fumes from the chemicals.

BE PREPARED

After an emergency, firefighters have to clean and check all their equipment (right) so they are ready to go the next time they are needed. Any equipment that is damaged during a fire has to be replaced before the next emergency.

TRACKED TRUCK

This European truck is used to get to fires in hard-to-reach places. It can drive through a muddy field, and even travel through rivers! Although they are small, the cabs of this truck can carry a team of firefighters and the equipment they need to tackle a blaze.

Foam tank

The rear cab holds a large tank for storing foam. Some fires can't be put out with water. When this happens, a special foam is used to cover the fire, preventing air from getting to it, which causes the fire to go out.

Equipment

There are fire extinguishers and breathing equipment in the front cab. It also holds stretchers and medical equipment.

Cab

The front cab is equipped with sirens, flashing lights, and a radio. It can carry three firefighters and the driver.

Tracks

Instead of wheels, this truck has tracks. These help it to drive over very rough ground.

FLYING IN

Sometimes the ground may be too rough even for this truck. If this happens, it can be picked up and flown to a fire by helicopter!

09 AY 01

UNUSUAL FIRES

Fires can pop up just about anywhere. When a forest or an oil well catches fire, special measures have to be taken. This may mean using a truck made for a special purpose or even sending in a robot to do the job! No matter what the situation, firefighters have to be prepared for anything.

FIRE SUIT

Very hot fires mean firefighters will need special safety gear to fight them. This suit (left) is made from aluminium, which protects firefighters from high-temperature fires by reflecting the heat from the flames. Like the chemical protectant suits (see page 17), these fire suits need special breathing equipment to get safe air to the firefighter.

OIL-WELL FIRE

At an oil-well fire, firefighters put up barriers to protect themselves (right). When they stand behind them, they are shielded from the heat of the flames.

GUARDING THE TUNNEL

Specially built fire trucks (above) are used in the Channel Tunnel, which runs between England and France. These drive down a rescue tunnel to reach a fire on a train.

FIRE MARSHAL

Racing cars can catch fire easily because they carry lots of fuel. As a result, car races have their own special firefighters (left). If there is a fire, they will put out the flames and rescue the driver.

ROBOT FIREFIGHTER

This robot firefighter (right) is used to get to fires that human firefighters couldn't reach. These could be in very small spaces or in places too dangerous for people.

FIRE TUG

Fire tugs fight fires on ships and oil rigs. They also tackle blazes that are on land at ports, harbors, and along rivers. The captain guides the boat close to the fire. The tug then pumps seawater or river water out through its water cannons. Water cannons spray massive jets of water over long distances.

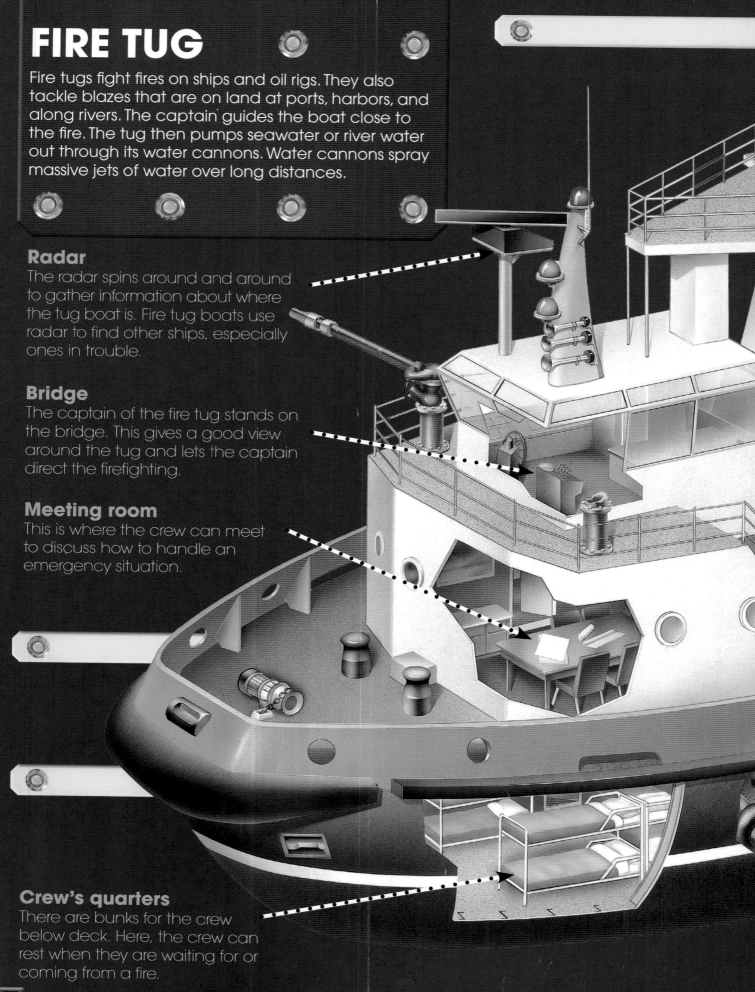

Radar
The radar spins around and around to gather information about where the tug boat is. Fire tug boats use radar to find other ships, especially ones in trouble.

Bridge
The captain of the fire tug stands on the bridge. This gives a good view around the tug and lets the captain direct the firefighting.

Meeting room
This is where the crew can meet to discuss how to handle an emergency situation.

Crew's quarters
There are bunks for the crew below deck. Here, the crew can rest when they are waiting for or coming from a fire.

Water cannons

The fire tug has several water cannons. These can be swiveled and moved up and down to shoot water at the blaze.

Water pump

The pump powers the fire extinguishers.

Lifeboat

The fire tug has its own lifeboat. The crew can lower it quickly into the water if the tug gets into a tight spot.

Engines

The fire tug has powerful engines. These push the boat through the roughest seas.

GOING THE DISTANCE

These water cannons (below) can shoot water up to the length of a football field!

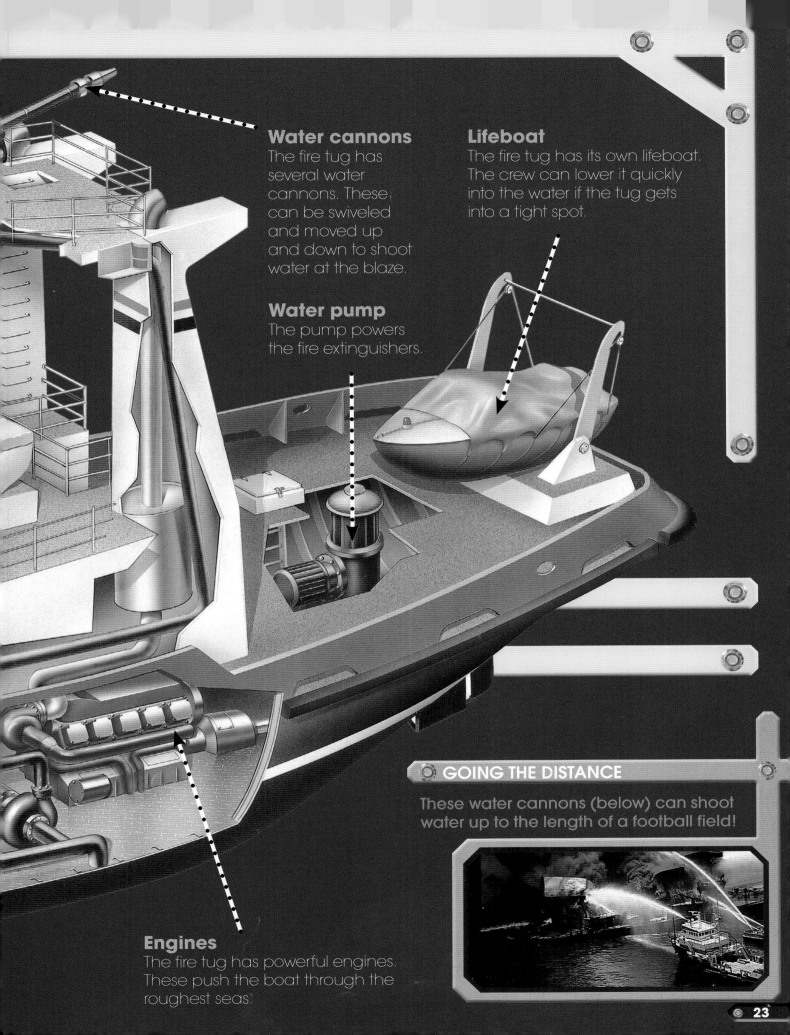

FIRES AT SEA

Machines at sea are full of gasoline and other highly flammable chemicals. These substances burn at high temperatures, making sea fires hard to put out with water. Sea firefighters must act quickly to save ship crews that may be trapped by a fire.

Crane

SUPPORT AT SEA

This huge craft (right) is called an Emergency Support Vessel (ESV). It is used to fight serious fires on oil rigs. It has helicopters to rescue people, and cranes to lift objects out of the water.

Water cannon

Lifeboat

Like fire tugs, the ESV carries lifeboats for emergency evacuation.

COAST GUARD

When a fire occurs on a small boat, the Coast Guard may respond to the alarm (left). They have fast boats that can rescue people before a blaze gets out of control.

Helicopter

Helicopters can be useful at sea when there isn't anywhere for firefighters to stand on the ship. They can drop water or fire retardant onto the blaze or they can lower firefighters onto a ship or lift people out.

OIL-RIG FIRES

Fires on oil rigs (left) are very fierce. This is because the oil and gas rush up from the seabed very quickly. This makes the fire very difficult to put out.

WATER CANNONS

The ESV is equipped with water cannons (right). These special hoses are similar to those on a fire tug (see pages 22-23).

Propeller

Instead of having wheels like a fire truck, the ESV has a propeller that helps the ESV move through the water.

Fuel

Fuel is carried in the flotation devices, called "pontoons."

POWERFUL JETS

The huge jets of water from a fire tug's cannons show how powerful its pumps are (left).

WATER BOMBER

An air tanker is an aircraft that can drop water or a fire retardant. It is used to fight forest fires, especially in areas that are hard to reach. The aircraft flies low and with one pass can spray water or the fire retardant substance over a large area of burning woodland. The tanker then returns to its airfield. Here, it refills its tanks with more fire fighting substance before flying back to fight the fire. This air tanker (right) drops a fire retardant over a forest. The substance suppresses the fire and provides a fertilizer to promote plant regrowth.

Fuel tanks
The aircraft carries fuel in tanks that are in its wings.

Engine
This water bomber has four engines. They are powerful enough to lift the plane when it is carrying water.

Cabin
The flight crew sits in the cabin. Behind this are bunks where they can rest.

Water tanks
Water is carried in huge tanks. These are carried in the water bomber's body.

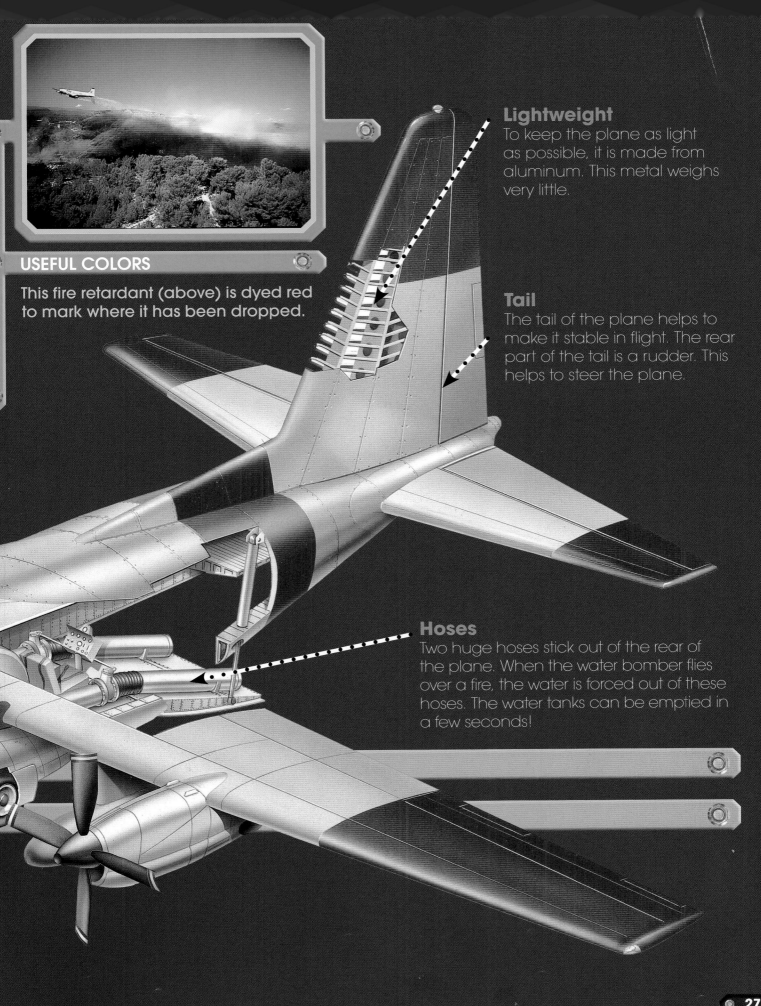

USEFUL COLORS

This fire retardant (above) is dyed red to mark where it has been dropped.

Lightweight

To keep the plane as light as possible, it is made from aluminum. This metal weighs very little.

Tail

The tail of the plane helps to make it stable in flight. The rear part of the tail is a rudder. This helps to steer the plane.

Hoses

Two huge hoses stick out of the rear of the plane. When the water bomber flies over a fire, the water is forced out of these hoses. The water tanks can be emptied in a few seconds!

FOREST FIRES

Sometimes forests catch fire. All of the plant life provides perfect fodder for a fire that can have natural causes, like a lightning strike. When this happens, firefighters have to take special precautions because large areas of wild land can burn up quickly. In the summer of 1988, a forest fire at Yellowstone National Park, Wyoming, burned about half the park's area. At one time, nearly 9,500 firefighters were working to tackle the blaze.

JUMPING INTO FIRES

Some firefighters are trained to parachute close to forest fires (left). This is useful when they are needed in a hurry at fires that are hard to reach.

STARTING FIRES

Some fires are started deliberately (right). By burning forest scrub in a controlled way, firefighters can prevent serious forest fires from spreading.

BEATING FIRES

Firefighters often try to beat out a forest fire with a fire beater (left). Though it looks like a garden rake, this handy tool goes a long way in putting out minor brush fires. The firefighter holds a long pole and uses the metal bristles at the other end to smother the fire. This is a good way to fight fires when water is unavailable.

Blades

The two separate sets of blades spin in different directions, helping the helicopter lift more weight.

HELICOPTERS

Helicopters can hover over the site of a fire. They drop water from a bucket, which they carry beneath (right).

Precise controls

The helicopter's ability to make a vertical take-off and landing can make it more useful than a plane during situations in tight locations.

Water bucket

The bucket can hold up to 2,600 gallons (9,842 liters) of water! It can get a refill from a nearby lake or river.

FOREST TRUCK

Special trucks carry firefighters to forest fires (left). They are built to drive over rough ground and weave in between trees. Their wide, tracked tires help them grip the wild terrain and their open sides allow the firefighters to jump out without worrying about opening a door between the trees.

GLOSSARY

Air tanker
An aircraft that can drop water or fire retardant spray onto a fire.

Breathing equipment (SCBA)
A device that supplies air to a face mask worn by firefighters. This lets them breathe while in a smoke-filled room.

Cabs
Compartments at the front or rear of a truck that carry drivers and sometimes other firefighters.

Coast Guard
One of the five American military services. The organization works to protect the personal safety of the people, the marine transportation and infrastructure, natural and economic resources, and the coast from attacks.

Crane
A device on rescue trucks for lifting heavy objects.

Deck gun
A special water outlet on top of a fire truck that can spray water a long distance.

Emergency Support Vessel (ESV)
A huge, floating platform that is used to fight fires on oil rigs.

Fire marshal
A special fireman who works at car races.

Fire retardant spray
This is a special spray made of chemicals that will smother a fire and prevent it from spreading. They often contain fertilizer that will help plant life regrow and are colored red so that firefighters can track where it has

Fire suit
A special suit made out of aluminium that is worn to protect firefighters in extremely hot fires.

Fire tug
Boats that fight fires on ships and oil rigs at sea.

Foam cannon
An airport truck device that aims foam at a fire.

Forest fire
A fire that takes place in a park or other location made of large areas of trees. The large amount of plant life makes these fires particularly dangerous and prone to spreading quickly.

Helicopter
A flying craft that can rescue people from or

Rescue truck
Firefighters use this truck to respond to lots of different emergencies, including rescuing people stuck in cars or underground.

Robot firefighter
A nonhuman firefighter used in small or dangerous spaces.

Steam engine
Early firefighting vehicles that were powered by steam and pulled by a team of horses.

Tiller truck
A fire truck that has to be steered from the rear as well as the front.

Track
A loop that runs around wheels, helping a vehicle travel over rough ground.

Siren
A device attached to a vehicle that makes a wailing sound. This warns people that firefighters are coming fast.

Stabilizers
Legs that keep the truck upright while the ladder is being used.

Turntable
The base on which the ladder rests. It allows it to turn in a circle.

Water cannon
A special device attached to a fire tug or ESV. It is used to point a jet of water at a fire.

INDEX

PHOTO CREDITS
Abbreviations: t-top, m-middle, b-bottom, r-right, l-left

Pages 5, 10b, 16t & b, 17t, 28t & b & 29b – Shout Pictures. 6t – Hulton Getty Collection. 7ml – Rex Features. 7mr, 11, 14b, 15t & b, & 19 – Angloco Ltd. 7b, 9 & 15m – Pierce Manufacturing. 10t, 25m & b – Eye Ubiquitous. 10m, 13, 20b, 21t & b, 23, 24b, 25t, 27, 28t & m – Frank Spooner Pictures. 16b – Spectrum Color Library. 17b – Science Photo Library. 21m – Empics.